THE JOURNEY OF LIFE

Life is a Beautiful Journey… Live It to the Fullest

Hema Peddibhotla

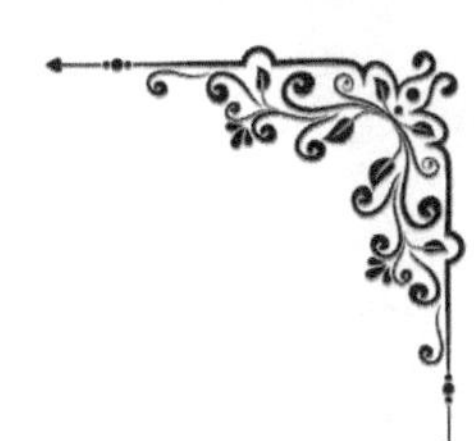

CONTENTS

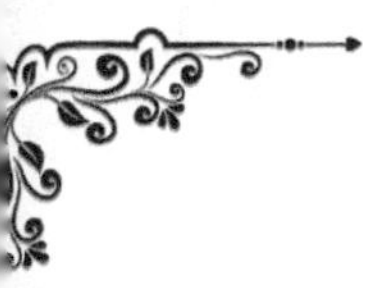

ACKNOWLEDGMENT

This Book is dedicated to each and every person who wants to understand the journey of a Human Life and understand how we are blessed with a human life and at every stage of our life we all have our unique journey and God has made each one of us, special in our own way, the only thing is we do not understand the beauty and gift given to all of this -"Precious Human Life" what we want this journey to be is in our own hands and enjoy this gift of life and enjoy this journey and make it such a beautiful one so that we all know what to do and what not to do during this journey.

Our experiences and lessons as we grow evolve and make us the best Version of ourselves. Understanding our unique journey and living it to the best is what makes our Life's Journey to reach our destination. All we need is to keep moving in right path.

GRATITUDE

This book is just a medium to pay my gratitude to all those who have played a vital role in my life. Through this book I want to thank each and every one of them.

God is Everywhere and invisible but still with our belief we can feel God's presence all around us.

Firstly, I want to Thank All Mighty for giving me this beautiful life and understand the essence and purpose of life. I thank god for everything in my life through his grace and blessings only I am writing this book. I am truly blessed.

In this path of journey, I want to thank My 'Spiritual Guru' Marcel Guruji – "Arun Shahastrabuddi" and Suresh Pai Guruji, who had given me spiritual knowledge and through their teachings and blessings I am evolving and growing as a better human being. I also thank my mentor/guru maa "Dr. Anjana Reetoria" has been always my source of inspiration and motivation. Through her teachings and her guidance, I am learning and evolving as a better Human Being each and every day.

Then first and foremost I want to thank My Mother Rajashree. G. Shurpali who brought me into this beautiful world and thought me how to live and

lead a confident life. It is her upbringing that has helped me, manage independently, she was my first teacher and my friend as I grew up and made me a person I am today. Thank You Mom for always loving me, supporting me, guiding me and motivating me.

Now I want to Thank my Father Gururaj. V. Shurpali who is a True Soldier as a Retired Flying Officer from Indian Air Force, he gave me the best upbringing and he is a source of strength and pillar to me and Family. He is a True Soldier of life and I want to Thank & Salute him from the bottom of my heart. He taught me one thing – "Never Give Up", I admire and respect him for the person he is always been contributing and adding value through serving selflessly till date at the age of 85 years he is very responsible and shows the Right Path to many through his guidance, Thank You Daddy.

I want to thank Geeta Shurpali who is my Aunt and has been a Motherly figure in my life. I could not have imagined my life without her support and guidance.

Now I want to thank both My Brothers for always loving me & supporting me. I want to Thank my Teachers/Gurus/Mentors who always have given me immense knowledge and contributed in my life.

I also want to thank my In-laws P. Kondala Rao & Sita Mahalakshmi/Brother-in-law - P. Ravi Kumar/ Co–sister – Asmita

For all the support and strength, I am truly blessed to have such Family where each and every individual has contributed and added value in my life's journey.

My In- laws have been true guidance and blessed and supported me in every aspect of life.

Now I want to thank the Most Important and Integrated Part of my life and that is none other than My Husband Mr. P Chandrasekhar who has always been supportive and understanding. If people say that only – There is a woman behind every man success, then I want to say that there is an understanding man behind every successful woman. I want to thank him for everything.

Now comes My Precious "Gift of God" that is none other than My Son – P Nilesh who is a precious gem and is an Excellent Son to Parents and a Wonderful Human- Being. He is My true companion/My good friend/My Critic/My strong opposition at times – when he wants me to be firm in my decisions, he plays a vital role in my life and I am truly blessed to be his Mother, So proud of him.

I want to thank my student Palak Jain who calls me "Guru Maa" has been a strength and motivation to be an Author. She is a loving daughter and supports me unconditionally.

I want to Thank All My Friends, Family, Relatives, Near and Dear ones and because of everyone today I am where I am in my life.

A Big Thank You to Indore City and Khajrana Ganeshji

I want to thank each and every student, who always have motivated me and called me an INSPIRATION.

A BIG THANK YOU to each and every one who has made my life so beautiful. THANK YOU EVERYONE.

CREDITS

Thanks

To

Sayali Vanjare

For her efforts to design Book Cover and All The Art Work done

THANK YOU

INTRODUCTION

"The Journey of Life "is a book, is a journey where every human being is gifted with the precious and beautiful LIFE and when we take birth and as we all grow there are different stages – (AGE) is our lives and how every person has their unique and special journey. We all learn & grow and learn our lessons in this life. We all have our own paths and experiences and different journey, and have our choices and decision. But how do they really make our journey beautiful one or not.

LIFE – LIVING INTENTIONALLY FOR EXCELLENCE.

How we learn, grow and evolve at different phases. We are the creators of our own life. While in this journey we all need to enjoy this beautiful journey and experience it and make this journey so beautiful and meaningful living it and celebrating and enjoying this Journey a worth living.

LIFE IS A BEAUTIFUL JOURNEY...............

Live it to the fullest.

Life is a beautiful journey that is cherished with happiness and joy. When we paddle our BOAT in this journey of life to reach to the other bank in the mid-way (middle) we may surmount pains and pleasures,

but we welcome them all with our courage and consistency.

If we give up, we may get drowned in the journey of life as there are deep waters of troubles i.e. challenges and tribulations. The obstacles or the speed–breakers are our lessons to learn. They teach us to become brave, bold and courageous. Life puts us in a difficult or challenging situations and tests our courage and endurance. There are moments of thrills and moments of grief in life which make the roller – coaster ride joyful, thrilling and satisfying.

When we paddle our BOAT to reach our 'destination' we witness all sorts of ups and downs (challenges and experiences) in life we have to become alert, prudent and efficient to climb up the ladder of Success.

Suppose we are preparing for an exam and if we get disheartened, we must keep our cool and face the dismal situation, and exploit another opportunity. Whenever the direction of wind is opposite, we apply a lot of force to paddle the boat in the same way no matter what adverse situation/circumstances we may face, we must not lose hope and perform our work/ deeds with utmost diligence.

To achieve Excellence, we have to groom ourselves and upgrade ourselves to get best results. Constantly polish our abilities and skills to live desired objective.

When we paddle our boat in the journey of life initially, we may find it hard, but we need to have patience & perseverance to succeed.

- LIFE ALWAYS WILL NOT BE FULFILLING.

We must accept life as it comes and keep striving with optimism then the journey of life become MEANINGFUL.

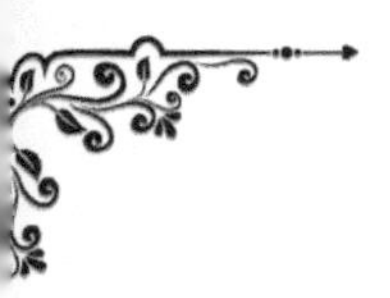

MY PURPOSE OF WRITING THIS BOOK

The purpose of writing this book is that life should be beautiful, meaningful and blissful. In this journey in initial growing phase of our life we are not knowing how to live life and during teenage the parents and children have their own pressures of life, and the distance between them and the gap between them -as working parents and children is increasing, as parents have 'money' but they do not have 'time'. This is the phase where the imbalance starts and to cope up with this 'Rat-Race' and "Competitive World" the adolescence age from (12 to 17 yrs.) are really not getting right direction and guidance, as there is no-one to whom they can talk and express as sometimes they are losing track and offtrack, clueless and without right direction (they get distracted).

So, this book of mine I want as a 'guiding tool' to every parent and children who are living a life which is forced on them due to our society and competitive world.

If through this book I am able to show some light so that a strong foundation can be laid upon in their early growing phases through right upbringing of the children. The parents are the first teacher specially

'MOM' and she can make the foundation so strong, that the child will have a strong pillar of values and conduct which should be inculcated from 6 months to 7 years. So, I am just giving a Road-Map (guiding tool), if anyone is having any Missing–link, in their life, they can just use this book as a Guiding tool, what have they missed upon and how can they take it further by moving in right direction.

We all have our own unique journey and path and everyone has come into this human form with a PURPOSE.

Purpose of living happy, healthy and a meaningful life.

If I can say that -The purpose of life is "To live life purposefully" adding value and meaning to life.

Through your experiences and learnings, you can evolve as better human being each day and every day. As the awareness of living a righteous life is not taught in schools, a holistic approach should be given to each one of us.

Life is all about learning, growing and evolving each day and every day.

Through this Book.

I have mentioned the various phases of life and how can we really live life with a purpose of living healthy, happy and meaningful life by balancing all aspects of our life.

In this journey As a Teacher and Life Coach, I have come across many people who want help and seeking for guidance, but they are not getting it in a righteous way, as through this book I am only guiding that in various phases of life, in our life–span, we are in such situation where in, are not able to seek help. I am only trying to guide (as a guiding tool) how can we all live rightfully and transform by laying a strong foundation on this journey of life – from Mother's Womb (Garbha Sanskar) till our last breath.

LIVING A MEANINGFUL LIFE, BY ADDING VALUE AND CONTRIBUTING TO SELF AND OTHERS.

'LIVE IT TO THE FULLEST'

CHAPTER 1

THE JOURNEY OF LIFE BEGINS FROM.............?
LIFE BEGINS FROM MOTHER'S WOMB

Do you think that the life begins or starts when we are born on to this earth as - "Human–Life"? Just think for a while ....!!

Did you feel something still connected to ....? Yes, you got it right, the journey of all our lives began 9 months prior to our birth, the journey of life began within our "Mother's Womb". Yes, we are growing in our Mother's Womb, each and every day, slowly and gradually.

It is a process where we are connected to our Mother through umbilical cord, through which we are fed and we are seeing, hearing and absorbing each and every thing (feelings, emotions, sanskars, nourishment, development) when we are in our Mother's Womb. Our Home for 9 months, where she keeps this tiny life, safe and protected, nurtures, and we see through the world, - from our Mother's eye. Whatever the Mother sees, reads, thinks, listens and watches the life inside absorbs each and every thing. That is the reason the mother during this phase, only does the good and divinely practices, so that the kid is given all those qualities which she is wanting the life in her is growing to become once born.

As we all have heard the story of "Abhimanyu" – This tells that Abhimanyu knew how to enter the 'ChakraYuh' from mother's womb only – as Abhimanyu heard this story in mother's womb. But when the story continued mother slept off and so he could not hear the entire story inside, he only knew to enter in, but did not know how to come out of ChakraYuh in the Battle Field (Kurukshetra).

Now days we are hearing "Garbha Sanskar" so often.

What does this mean?

Garbha Sanskar is a process during 9 months the mother listens, watches, hears and speaks about Sanskar (qualities) she wants in her child, and starts cultivating these from womb during her 9 months of beautiful journey, within a new life inside her, which she starts to inculcate these Sanskar through her as the life inside is able to grasp and absorb each and every thing and starts to learn from Mother's Womb.

So, this learning and growing each day and evolving starts from within Mother's Womb.

That is why the Human Creation is the most beautiful creation of God.

Learning .... -> Growing .... -> Evolving each day at every phase.

This beautiful connection between mother and the life within they share each and everything together, and that is why this journey within also each day is so beautiful. The 9 months over, then new journey begins from here.

Even during the Birth, The mother undergoes pain - to give birth to the life inside and that life within also puts all efforts and undergoes the process along with mother to come out -> The young life also fights and finally makes the way to the beautiful world outside and is then born. Now the individual existence starts, as soon as the chord is cut and the new journey of life begins on this beautiful -Mother Earth (Dharti Par Aagman).

But the journey started 9 months prior only, before birth that is inside Mother's Womb.

Every life has to undergo this journey and is one of the most beautiful journeys which cannot be seen from outside but can be felt within each and every moment.

Undergoing pain to see the final outcome and a beautiful outcome is "one life giving life to another life". Becoming a mother is a biggest Gift of God to every woman.

So, in this manner like inside also we were learning, growing, evolving and after birth also, we keep learning, growing and evolving each and every day to make this journey beautiful and amazing.

Garbha Sanskar being practised now a days has been passed to us from generations (from our ancestors).

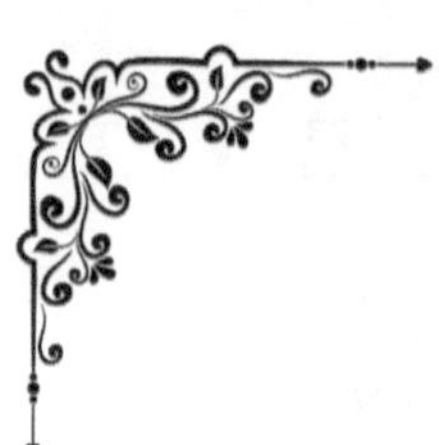

CHAPTER 2

HUMAN BIRTH – GIFT OF GOD TO US

As we all are been so blessed and gifted with this precious "HUMAN LIFE ".

LIFE – A precious Gift of God to us.

AGE – (TODDLERS TO YOUNG CHILDREN)

As we take birth, and grow as a toddler we are so pure and innocent, we just live and enjoy each and every moment of our life, as we are taken care by our parents/ loved ones and relatives. A happy and carefree life with lots of love and laughter as we are seeing through the lens of God's most Innovative and beautiful creation of that Almighty Supreme who made us – we all are God's most unique and best creations. But as we grow that is when we start going to kindergarten, KG1/ KG2 and further schooling, as before going to school the parents are the first "TEACHER" of every child, so they learn everything from them good and bad both. The parents are first teachers and the house is the first school of every child as to what they see what they hear they pick up very fast and they develop good and bad habits-from parents and loved ones. So here now I want to say and tell that every one's upbringing, cultures may vary and differ from one another, but the foundation of everyone's life is the same, that the foundation should be very strong and every parent need to lay a strong foundation. Each parent always tries to give their best to their children in regard with their social parameters and cultures of the society. But the most important thing I want to say and emphasis here is that on the blank paper of the innocent minds (children) whatever we are printing becomes a blueprint of their life and on this foundation the building is laid upon. So now as an Author I am not judging any parent here, but want to only make my point very clear that teach and imbibe the qualities you want your child to inculcate and replicate – so be very careful on the words you speak, the way you are speaking "tone and politeness". So, from here only the journey of the innocent minds (lives) begins.

What the child requires the most now is the precious time and love of parents & family, try to spend a quality time every day without fail, irrespective of your busy schedules and professional life, take out some time only for them. This is my humble request to every parent that at this phase your time is more precious than your money (time is more important as well as money to give best life to your kid). This may now sound very silly to most of the people, but definitely the impact on the child's mind cannot be seen. Every child is a reflection of their parents – looks, nature, habits, behaviour......all.

So not only the duty is over just by sending them to school and getting homework done, but what are you really making your children........? A mechanical robots and doing the same thing every day (the intention should be overall their brain intellect and overall other activities too should also be looked upon)

A proper Mental and Physical exercise should be given to them and making things loving and enjoyable, so that they are not felt to be forced, but in a very fun and loving way parents should get involved in this way. Every child requires attention and care at this stage. Make loving, sharing and caring as their natural way of living. I am here trying only to say that -in this busy hectic and automated technological world young kids from the age of 3 to 5 years are occupying more of screen space, more than fun loving indoor games and toys, so that primarily each child will only get diverted by indulging them in some activities like -story-telling, rhymes, poems, playing some games with them indoors, colouring, which involves some physical movements also. In such way a balanced, healthy upbringing foundation with good manners and etiquettes should be the foundation, which begins at home and should be inculcated from childhood only like -saying prayers before eating food, saying Thank You to food, clothes, toys, school, teachers, friends this will become habit of child. Developing good habits in their early phase. "Prayers" and "Thank You" (Gratitude- being thankful and grateful) is a basic foundation and then later on as they grow in age and classes (higher classes) Teach them breathing technique. Taking deep breaths (Inhale and exhale) Yoga and exercising for 5-10 mins in the morning before they live for their school.

For overall physical and mental development and growth (well-being).

Along with their academics this is very essential in today's world as even the children are just running in the monotonous busy life and they are not taking time in such activities (for mental and physical well–being).

I request every parent not to put too much pressure on their academics/grades and ranking, as each child has their own unique talent and each one is Gifted with (inborn talent) so here is what every parent need to observe their child unique qualities /talents as can be easily identified by every parent. Try to encourage them in that particular field in which they are good at, as this may not be necessarily a part of their academics sometimes, (do not try to supress them). As always academics will comes first and then encouraging simultaneously

So, by the time the child is of the age-10 years the parents do not realise that a blue-print is laid out on to their minds (brain) and heart (feelings and emotions) but due to fear they do not communicate and express themselves to parents/elders/teachers or relatives. As this is the age where they are like a mud/clay (pottery) whatever shape you give and the, mould you give to them they will be shaping and moulding into them.

Till now I have only been telling at this age, why the children must be given them into their inheritance is-because this is where the turning point and shaping up takes place.

I have seen in my life many times the child is suffocating and getting frustrated, but unable to address it and this reflects on their behaviour and well- being of the child. Even the bright and balanced happy and physically fit and energetic child now gets metamorphosised into a different personality.

Academically doing fantastic and excelling but trying to run away with reality and harsh truth of their lives and then here sometimes the route or the path which is right for them is being en-routed now to a different path, and somewhere their journey here gets deviated at times due to the external factors, pressures, environment, competition and upbringing too.

As children at this age are too tender and are not in a position to understand what is good or bad and they get carried away at times.

Here is the turning point of this phase of life as children and as WE are a crucial part of their journey (WE here mean – parents, relatives, teachers, friends, society where we live in). All play their role and contribute towards making this journey easier and enjoyable or making it a tough one by changing the routes and path.

Here is what I want to tell all the parents/teachers/ elders to really understand the young and tender minds and emotions to help them and maintaining a balance by talking and communicating to them and making them understand and maintain a balance (physical and mental wellness) as this is missing now a days in this fast-moving technological world, where we all are just in race, just wanting to win the race anyhow.

I want to say that each child is a unique child with unique qualities of their own which we need to identify them, very minutely without judging and comparing to others to bring out their best hidden talents and some skills they have, but went un-noticed in -"Rat-Race" and competition in academics and grades – the young minds at the age of 10 years are too young for expressing what is going inside them, and due to fear just keep on doing without liking it to do – due to which at times, their mental wellness reflects on their physical being -so here I am just asking to maintain balance for overall well-being and betterment for their growing phase. Sometimes physical and mental balance are neglected and reflects on their overall well-being as they grow.

As now here I am just wanting to bring to notice, by only focusing on one thing in this phase is 'foundation' which we are laying the building of their bright "FUTURES" so lay the foundation strong, so that building of their future is strong and tall (bright and prosperous future).

KEY POINTS FOR BASIC FOUNDATION TO KIDS

- PARENTS – BEST FRIEND /TEACHER/WELL-WISHERS
- HOME – FIRST SCHOOL OF EVERY CHILD

- QUALITY TIME – SPEND ATLEAST 30 TO 40 MINUTES QUALITY TIME WHICH IS FUN AND ENJOYABLE WITHOUT FAIL'
- MANNERS AND ETTIQUETTES TO BE TAUGHT IN A FUN – LOVING AND JOYFUL WAY.
- MAKE LEARNING – A FUN-LOVING WAY
- INCULCATING GOOD HABITS FROM CHILDHOOD.
- PRAYER BEFORE EATING FOOD.
- SAYING THANK YOU FOR WHATEVER THEY ARE GETTING THROUGH LOVE.
- STORY TIME BEFORE SLEEPING:

NICE SHORT STORIES – WITH MORALS AND VALUES

- PHYSICAL AND MENTAL PLAYFUL AND FUN-LOVING GAMES & EXERCISES.

SOME PHYSICAL PLAYTIME IS MUST.

- SELF-DESCIPLINE AND DEDICATED TIME FOR STUDIES ARE MUST.
- HOBBIES -INTERESTS AND WHAT THEY ARE GOOD AT AND LOVE TO DO.
- SAY NO TOO MUCH OF SCREEN-TIME TV/ MOBILE

REDUCE SCREEN TIME FOR EYES AND GIVE IN A DAY A LIMITED 15 MINS PERIOD PER DAY.

- SOME INDOOR GAMES–BUILDING BLOCKS, MISSING PIECES TO BE COMPLETED, CHESS, SCRABBLE, SOLVING PUZZLES,

BRAIN DEVELOPING GAMES.

- MAKE THEM LEARN CYCLING OR SWIMMING AT A VERY EARLY AGE (3 TO 7 YEARS)

BEST FOR PHYSICAL WELL BEING -TO BE HEALTHY AND FIT

- BREATHING EXERCISES – YOGA AND FOR OVERALL DEVELOPMENT (FOR HEALTHY MIND AND BODY)

{PHYSICAL EXERCISE + MENTAL EXERCISE = HEALTHY AND HAPPY MIND, BODY}

- GOOD AND HEALTHY EATING HABITS.

NOT PAMPERING MUCH FOR FAST FOODS, CHOCOLATES AND COLD-DRINKS

- GIVE THEM YOUR:
  - LOVE
  - TIME
  - CARE

- SUPPORT

- GUIDANCE

UNDERSTAND AND COMMUNICATE WITH THEM.

• DO NOT BE STRICT WITH KIDS. MAKE IT FUN AND LOVING SO THEY ENJOY DOING IT.

Young tender innocent minds and their hearts are just like a clay and the parents are the potters to mould and give their life a proper shape which they want, but very delicately and handling with gentleness so that they do not break. As we have seen that when we sow seeds into the mind and then their shoots up a tiny pod out of that which is later on given proper care, sunlight, water and fertilizers so that they bloom into a healthy plant. Similarly, we all elders are responsible towards the nourishment and growth of these young minds so they are transformed and moulded into a beautiful teenager as they grow up, by nourishing them with love, care, compassion, kindness, humility, happiness, proper environment, giving them morals and core values like respect, discipline, courage, confidence, as these core values should be given from a young toddler and this become their habits and lifestyle as they grow up with these values. They learn from the environment and surroundings too, so which can be sometimes have an impact and reflect upon their behaviour and character, so we need to see that if sometimes they do pick up some good or bad, then to make them understand with a proper reasoning will help them to realise why they should not repeat it once again and they can be managed at a beginning and initial stage with love and proper guidance and will help them to be more creative. As they are growing their overall growth (mentally and physically) should have a balance. So, they enjoy everything and grasp things in a better way. It is in our hands how we want our children to be at this stage, as they are too tender and they are the reflection of parents/teachers/ elders/ family and society.

So, each one of us are directly or indirectly contributing in building and shaping up their overall growth and their lives.

SUGGESTIONS:

Each one of us should take a conscious responsibility to shape the young minds in nurturing them the right way in their early stages only as they easily grasp good or bad both and develop them.

This stage is the foundation we are laying out their building (bright future).

In this journey of all our lives, we all start from the same point that is our birth- coming into this beautiful world as human lives but each one's destination will be different depending on how are they living this life with right way of living will decide their final further journey.

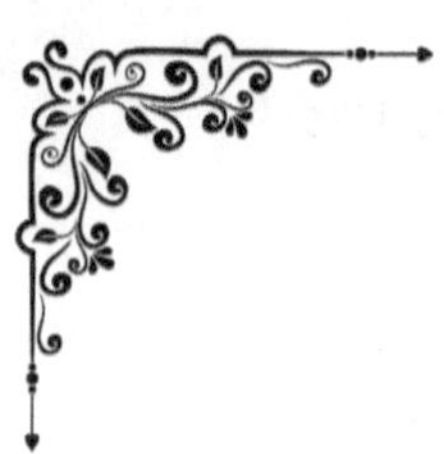

CHAPTER 3

ADOLESCENCE INNOCENT YOUNG MINDS AND TEENAGERS

This phase of life is the most beautiful and transformative journey in each one of our lives. This phase is very delicate and tender as adolescence phase they have innocent young minds.

I will say that now the young minds understand things, but sometimes are not able to know whether that is good or bad. As still they are in their transformative phase.

As we all grow in our age we grow up with our limitations and certain boundaries. Now at this age the balancing between academics, personal life and friends all needs to be looked upon, from the point of young minds and also parental point of view. Generally, at this age all the young minds are loving be more playful and they are now on the other hand been burdened with the pressure and excelling in their academic life and which they do it forcibly, as they are now having their own likes and dislikes. They try to impose their views, opinions, emotions and feelings as they are not able to balance between both. Parents also now a days due to high aspirations try to overload the young minds with coaching and additional learning to lead in the competitive race. By the time this mechanical robotic life becomes a part of their living and growing.

Here comes a phase where at some point of time they start to show their difference of opinion and they are not allowed to do so. So, the initial fights start at the age of 13 to 15 years, as they want their freedom, space and choices to be made on their own, but on the other hand the parents have their own view, so here is the gap between teenagers and parents. This gap between them can be said as Generation Gap. As the young children are neither too young nor they are adults too. So, their decision-making skills are not on the basis of what is good/bad it is on basis of "comparison" and "freedom" given to them.

Every young mind has some physical transformation also in their growth period now. So now they want to cope with the worldly pressure as they have to excel in their academics (Xth Std to XIIth Std) the turning point of their lives.

They have to decide which path to choose, but at times the DECISIONS of their future are taken by parents/ relatives and family. Which may be according to their will and wish or sometimes be against their will and wish.

They are now showing up their personalities through their behaviours and core values of lives. Many young teenagers at this point of their life gets deviated from their path as there is a war between internal world and the external world too. They now at this transformative stage of their lives want to be their own DECISION MAKERS of their lives. Here is where now the small fights between parents and children starts showing up on much higher level which turns into argument now slowly and gradually. But now comes where their future is dependent on decisions.

The most of the young teenagers in this growing stage tend to hide things and do not share with parents. What I am here wanting and requesting to everyone is that not communicating with the young minds and understanding them is the mistakes many do and the bridge of "faith" is broken between them and the main important thing which comes is as elders they feel that their respect and fine line of human ego comes where the relationships starts weakening up and the balance and direction to which should have been leading them becomes a 'judgement' on them, (teenagers).

The communication, mutual understanding and wellbeing (mental + physical) are the key areas during this phase of life, where this journey together can be so pleasant and joyful, may sometimes get tough as they move forward.

As we now moving forward in this journey we all are undergoing different phases of life and each one of us have our own journey by the choices we make and decisions we take, at this cross roads decides the place where we want to go or how we want to go. I am trying to explain our journey through different phases like toddlers, teenagers, youth, mid aged and old age. But at every phase we are learning, growing and evolving in our lives. Through our experiences and lessons learnt.

"LEARN FROM YOUR MISTAKES" AND RECTIFY

BUT ON THE OTHER HAND, WANT TO SAY DO NOT --- "MIS TO TAKE"………..

The evolution during this journey determines our destiny (destination – where you want your life to be).

The Academics/Professional front does not define a human's potential and calibre. We should not judge them by the marks or grades they have got, but we should judge them by their qualities, Inbuilt talents, their strength, skills they have is what really defines them.

So, the main and very crucial part in this phase of life, friendship and communication between a teenagers and parents needs to be strengthened and becoming their "BEST FRIENDS" sharing their thoughts, views, opinions, and respecting their point of view (view point). This journey can be enjoyed through companionship, quality time, Expressing and talking (both the sides–both ways) hearing and doing what is right and would be for the betterment of self and overall.

Do not decide their future or career streams depending on the grades and competition. Just be relaxed – If someone is choosing something for them, because they have chosen it don't choose and put yourself into the dark–tunnel where you have entered in but you do not know how to move forward (as unable to see and analyse the path in darkness). Sometimes entering is very easy, but to come out of that tunnel becomes too difficult and sometimes impossible.

The labelling of each one takes place by evaluating them and putting in different categories.

This phase of life is a turning point in this journey and sometimes the deviations in this phase can be the pot holes and speed breakers on this journey. So, choose and decide wisely.

SUGGESTIONS/KEY TAKEAWAYS:

As every phase of human life is an everyday process of growing. The human body (physical growth) only grows up to a certain age which is from (Birth till 18 years – 21 years). Their mental growth, physical health, emotional health and overall well-being undergoes a physical transformational phase and from 10 to 19 years is the phase, where we humans are having many physical and emotional changes too in them. As the elders are not feeling free to talk to teenagers at this stage they should be very friendly in explaining the various changes, at these phases of lives they are new to the changes, as the young minds are unable to cope, share or ask about this openly so "Awareness" has to be created in a society. Where we live in, we should be open to talk on these sensitive issues /topics are the teenagers are undergoing many emotional and physical changes. So, this phase of life is very delicate in physical, mental, emotional and educational aspects. All needs to be "balanced" as sometimes the changes may cause a positive or negative impact in their growing stage.

BALANCE

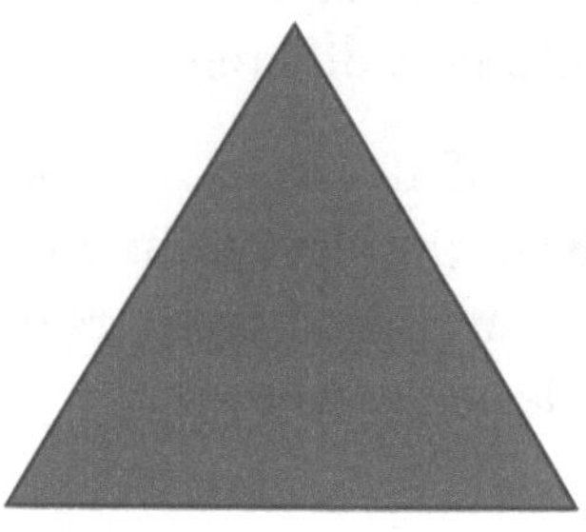

CHOOSING WISELY WHAT YOU WANT AND TAKING/CHOOSING THAT AS YOUR "CAREER" IS WHAT "DECIDES" YOUR FUTURE……………………..

CHOOSING YOUR CAREER – WHAT YOU LOVE TO DO.

KNOWING LIKES AND DISLIKES and doing what you like to do. Following your passion to be successful in life.

This phase is a blooming stage (phase) of life. As a bud is blooming into a beautiful "flower" so the young lives are transforming into beautiful youth from teenager. So, this metamorphosis in each has its unique experience and transformations, but all they need is a proper environment, guidance, support.

Aspirations and Dreams are now - to on their peak but to bring them into reality is – doing right things at right time and balancing every aspect of life i.e. family, friends, academic progress. If one aspect also is imbalanced then the journey and path gets deviated.

Prioritising your likes and interests – Roadmap to your future reality.

Follow Do's and Don'ts so that – boundaries setting and following the life path with instructions will lead to right destination where one wants to reach (how to reach is in your hands).

3C'S OF LIFE: CHOICES, CHANCES AND CHANGES.

"YOU MUST MAKE A CHOICE TO TAKE A CHANCE IF YOU WANT ANYTHING IN LIFE TO CHANGE".

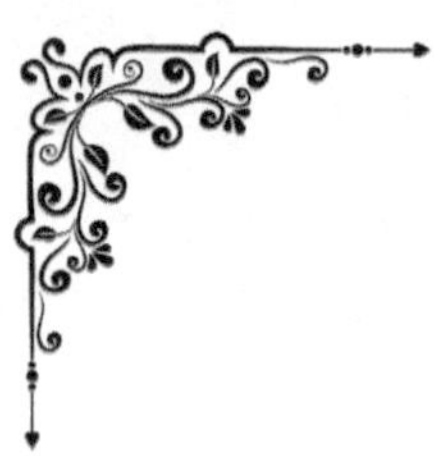

CHAPTER 4

THE YOUTH AND MID – AGE

This phase of life is when the teenagers are now transforming into "youth" and further youth to mid-age (phase of life).

Life is a 'Vehicle' and in this vehicle called life all the "FOUR WHEELS" – HEALTH

RELATIONSHIP

CAREER

MONEY

- NEEDS TO BE BALANCED (For Easy and Smooth Journey of Life).

This is the phase a young mind with young physique is trying to figure out things as at age, as they are the creators of their own lives. Wanting to create a life of what they want and desire, where now they are facing the reality of life. The gap between their dreams to reality is the journey they must take. Dreams into reality as all the 4 aspects in this journey of our life are and balancing is what makes their journey beautiful and amazing.

In each human life these are the aspects:

A) HEALTH (Physical, Mental and Emotional)

B) RELATIONSHIP (Personal Life)

C) CAREER/JOB

D) FINANCIAL LIFE (Money)

All are connected and dependent on one another.

- Note: if one aspect of life gets disturbed the other aspects of life have an impact.

WAY OF LIVING: HOW ARE YOU LIVING AND WHAT ARE YOU "LEAVING".

This is the phase of life where in a youth is responsible for the choices, decisions, career, relationships, and financial aspects. In other words, "Youth is the creator of their own lives" as we are god's most beautiful creation but to make this creation of our life is in our hands and in our minds.

Some of the paths are smooth and some paths are not easy as one has to overcome all the situations of life and balancing every area of our life, we need to learn lessons and evolve as a better version of self, as the challenging situations are building blocks of our life.

Here I want to emphasise on one fact very much as we human- beings are given a superior mind, and by using our brains and giving our best will determine the kind of life we are living.

As we are now talking about the journey and this phase of our life determines (foundation) of building our future. So, everyone passes out from their 10 + 2 and College degree. Now the challenge of getting a Job or starting own business, choosing stream (10+2)

- CHOOSE A CAREER YOU ARE GOOD AT (SCIENCE, ENGINEERING or MEDICAL, COMMERCE, ARTS, COMPUTER SCIENCE ETC) OR THE FIELD WHICH YOU WANT TO PURSUE FURTHER.
- ➤ CHOOSING AND DECISION (decision making)

Do not choose a career because Family, Friends or a Close Friends are pursuing to compete/ compare with others and just decide which is good for you – you are good in it. Have interest or passion to pursue, as this only will decide where you want to go (Focus), how you want to do, what is best for you...........?

Ask yourself which is very important.

- What is that "YOU "want to do?
- Why "YOU" want to do? (is it your passion or you want to follow the trend)
- What is that you are good at?
- Which are the talent and skills you might have as a second option (milestone)
- How you want to go about it (decided path)
- How long will it take to complete (Time frame & Eligibility {AGE})
- If any Burning issues/obstacles what are those burning issues/obstacles that hold you back.

- Who is "RESPONSIBLE" for your choices and decisions?

Who is RESPONSIBLE FOR YOUR LIFE?

- What is the "Purpose" Behind?

Everyone as a human – being has been assigned a purpose in life – living a life with PURPOSE.

What is your "PURPOSE"?

Just to live and go which is just making a living (livelihood).

OR

You are "DESIGNER OF YOUR OWN LIFE "

You will design it so beautifully that your good deeds and work you did for others and world through your contribution will be remembered even after you leave this world (Leave a legacy).

By adding value and contributing in whatever way you can and whatever you are good at.

Finding your true "POTENTIAL" and being "PASSIONATE" doing in whatever you are good/best at, will determine your SUCCESS.

"FOLLOW YOUR PASSION, MONEY AND SUCCESS WILL FOLLOW YOU".

RE-INVENT (re- invent yourself)

Re-invent - of all creations of God, human being alone is an "evolving consciousness" i.e. we can consciously evolve.

Example: At the age of 45 can wake up in the morning as Mohandas Karamchand Gandhi…. Can re-invent a Mahatma Gandhi within by the end of the day.

Example: Agnes – Mother Teresa, Agnes can re-invent as Mother Teresa.

RE-INVENTING YOURSELF, is

"RENEWING YOUR PERCEPTION" – Re-invent myself.

➢ DIRECTION OF YOUR LIFE AT AGE 22 YRS – 45 YRS.

BY THE MID AGE OF YOUR LIFE

2 DECADES (THIS IS THE GOLDEN PERIOD OF LIFE)

- What else should be the 'focus' of my life?
- How do I expand my boundaries of what I can reach out for life?

For all the Potential I have discovered about myself in the last over 2 decades.

- WHAT ELSE SHOULD BE MY EXPECTATION FROM LIFE?

FAMILY – CELEBRATION OF IMPERFECTION IS CALLED "FAMILY."

Family is a place where imperfections is seen, but it is not felt.

RELATIONSHIPS – TO MAINTAIN A BALANCE BETWEEN WORK & PERSONAL LIFE.

In the past 2 decades (20 Yrs.)

The basis of Relationship has been shifted from Emotions to Information (people are more dependent on information and social media)

Any relation to grow and flourish requires 2 important things:

1. Investing your time

2. Communication

"That on which you INVEST TIME AND COMMUNICATION always grows ".

That on which you do not give your time and communication will shrink and die.

In any relationship whether it is parents and kids, husband and wife, colleagues, friends, neighbours (anyone) purely based on the EMOTIONS, you don't feel intimate close or a sense of ownership towards anybody -anymore

Your emotional intelligence and values have no place. So it is very important that Reinventing yourself, for becoming the best version of self.

RE-INVENT EVERY ASPECT OF YOUR LIFE!

- HEALTH
- PERSONAL RELATIONSHIP
- PROFESSIONAL RELATIONSHIP, COLLEAGUES AND BOSS.
- FRIENDS AND RELATIVES.

Have a healthy and harmonious relationships.

TO BE - "HUMAN" IS HUMANITY.

To look at everyone with love & harmony, try to spread positivity and peace and make this world together a beautiful place to live.

BALANCING ALL THE 4 ASPECTS OF LIFE IS VERY IMPORTANT:

1. HEALTH (PHYSICAL & MENTAL HEALTH)

2. RELATIONSHIP (PERSONAL, PROFESSIONAL & SOCIAL RELATIONSHIP)

3. CAREER (CHOOSING AND DOING WHAT YOU ARE GOOD IN AND MAKE A PROSPEROUS CAREER IN THE SAME FIELD).

4. MONEY (THIS IS VERY IMPORTANT PART OF EVERYONE'S LIFE AS THIS GIVES YOU LIVE A BETTER AND COMFORTABLE LIFE.

(*IF THIS IS NOT THEIR THE OTHER 3 ASPECTS INDIRECTLY GETS IMPACTED)

Having a right mindset determines your direction in which you will navigate and make decisions on your thinking.

IDENTIFY WHO/WHAT IS INFLUENCING YOUR THINKING ?

ALWAYS SURROUND YOURSELF WITH RIGHT – MINDED PEOPLE "SANG KA RANG" (Power of Association).

As they say that you are a reflection of group of people you are associated with. Your good association with your friends/colleagues and closed one either will elevate your standards of thinking and living or will pull you down as you have been draining due to your wrong association and choices.

"IF YOU ARE SITTING WITH 5 IDIOTS, YOU ARE THE 6TH ONE" AND "IF YOU ARE SITTING WITH 5 SUCCESSFUL PEOPLE YOU ARE THE 6TH ONE".

My Mentor Anjana Reetoria always says.

Here I want to make one thing very clear that every person, is what -CHOICES AND DECISIONS they make in their life. Your choices and decisions you take in this phase of life will determine your path and journey to where you want to reach. So never depend on anyone and take other's opinion and suggestions as you are the driver of your life, so do not allow anyone else to control your vehicle be on the driving seat and have the control on stearing and drive to destination where you want to reach.

If it is a career to choose, college to choose, which stream to choose, or which career options you want to take and pursue should not be on the basis of family and friends, but it should be just – what you want to do ?why you want to do? How passionate are you for doing it? Believing in yourself and giving your best will make your journey more interesting exploring and will love your every aspect towards what you thought & decided to make it true. Your RIGHT ACTIONS are what determines your future and destiny. I want to say that life is a "bicycle"where we have to keep our balance and keep moving and in this journey there is no STOP/PAUSE we have to balance and keep moving. So everyone has their own unique talent, interests, passion and this uniqueness is only identified by evaluating in what we are good,what we love to do & so need to choose only that.You have that potential in yourself,do not compare yourself with anyone as you are unique and make your own "IDENTITY". Forcing yourself to do, as just that will give you a livleyhood,will only make you a mechanical robot in today's fast evolving technological world/era.

This phase of life is turning point and "golden period" of everyone's life.Making and shaping our life is in our hands as there is a famous saying - "YOU ARE THE CREATOR OF YOUR OWN LIFE". Make it meaningful and beautiful by creating a life worth living.

As the journey of our life is full of learning and growing and to be evolved. Each day we are all given the same number of hours and time but how we use that is in our hands and in our minds. As we want to live our dream life but only few fulfill their dreams and live their dream lives. Do you know the reason why ? I know you must be thinking and saying its sheer luck that's why they are lucky. Its not the truth the only difference between them (the successful and Common people) Is that they do right things at the right time and they do learn from their mistakes and convert that into an opporunity.

Accepting the challenge and converting it into opportunities is what successful people do, they evolve and grow from their experiences and lessons.

So what a person thinks and believes is what they become.

As I said that this phase of human journey it's the most important and the beautiful one.

As here a young man becomes a 'gentleman' and young girl becomes a 'woman'. As a person grows physically and mentally too this is also the age of hormonal changes, emotions,buliding up harmonious relationship,finding a partner, getting settled in life, balancing personal and professional lives, Balancing social lives priortising responsibilties and to grow in family too, having kids and their upbringing.The series of so many different/various events occur in this beautiful phase of life (Youth).

The one who knows to balance all the four aspects of life through right timely actions and deeds are full of life and enjoy their journey, but some who get distracted in between their journey get deviated and imbalanced due to negiligence of their untimely deeds and not enjoying their journey -as they do not learn their lessons and create a undesired life unknowingly and unwantingly.

Most of the life lessons are into this phase only. As we humans grow we are always wanting to make our own choices and decision but sometimes getting carried away and get influenced by the external factors like parents/relatives/friends and social community influences and we are just trying to please everyone and not knowing what actually you are wanting out of life? What impacts here is sometimes a person opts for a career/college which one doesn't want to pursue. Gets into a company -job,where one is not wanting to work, but still continues as one has to earn for family and take care of the responsibilities.

QUALITY OF LIFE – (YOUR THINKING

CIRCUMSTANCES AND ENVIORNMENT DETERMINES IT).

When we are in a growing stage from our adolesence to teenagers we are still very tender and cannot differentiate between what is right/good for us or what is not good/right so we are like 'clay' and get moulded into the shape of mould. But as we have now finished college and grown up young brains, body and mind we have our thought process and we are taking decisions for self. So you the designer of your own life, design it so beautifully that you are not having any regrets for paths choosen and should grow,explore and evolve as a better human beings. The first responsibility of yours is towards 'SELF' that is to have a balanced life (health, personal life, professional life, financial life). If any one always is out of alignment then the path of life becomes challenging. Lets now discuss about the first aspect of life:

A) HEALTH

'HEALTH IS WEALTH'

Every person irrespective of the age has to be healthy, fit and fine and energetic.

As we all have a very busy lifestyle from our schooling days onwards, just life has been so robotic and mechanical that we are not finding enough time for our physical and mental fitness.

Health here plays a very important role in everyone's life. If you are wealthy, but if you are not having physical and mental fitness you cannot enjoy that wealth, irrespective of how wealthy one may be. So here being healthy only doesn't mean physical fitness like going to gym or doing high intensity workouts it means that one should have a proper physic and fitness. For this everyone needs to take out some time from busy schedule if possible in the morning and practice few habits which will keep you healthy.

CAN FOLLOW ANY OF THESE:

- Early morning brisk walking
- Sit in a quiet place and practice deep breathing exercises (inhale and exhale) for 15 to 30 mins
- Do yoga as this will keep you fit and will give you healing too.
- Meditation - closing your eyes for 15-20 mins and focusing on "om" or any relaxing music will give you calmness.
- 30 minutes to 1 hour Zumba dancing (is a great way to exercise) in the morning just moving your body and the blood circulation will always keep you fit and healthy.
- If you can join "gym" under a guidance of a trainer you will attain a good healthy lifestyle.

People now days are so busy in their hectic schedule that they do not have time for themselves, that is why people are not able to balance their physical fitness and mental fitness. Now why is it's so important to maintain a balance between them? As we are now a days living in a more stressful life and this leads to many mental illnesses like - Anxiety, panic attacks and sometimes "depression". Here if a person is not able to manage stress daily this will also reflect on the person's physical health and slowly small things take a form of disease like - Blood pressure, diabetes, obesity, thyroid, PCOD in ladies and many more. So why don't we start taking care of ourselves thinking that this is our basic responsibility and everyone's becomes aware about well- being of our own body/ mind by nourishing it with healthy balanced diet (AVOID JUNK FOOD) and do physical exercise (gym or cycling or swimming) and mental exercise (like yoga and meditation) will help you leading a balanced healthy life. So, let's make this is our priority to take care of "self" (self-care).

As there is a famous quote

"Health is wealth"

Our health is real wealth.

From the Time, we are in the Mother's Womb, we are been fed through mother and the overall development of a child is dependent on mother, so if she is healthy the child is Healthy. Now after the child comes on this earth, after the birth now has its own individual existence and survival- physically and mentally. In the early phase, the child is totally dependent on Mother's feed and after few months the baby is given baby food and as the child grows, every organ needs to be healthy, so for this a balanced Nutritious diet is much essential to keep body healthy. Physically in growing Stage the mothers are taking care of the diet, but as we grow our Health is our own responsibility. But in this busy sedentary life, everyone is so much tied up that they neglect their physical and Mental Health. As we all have 24 Hrs, We have to maintain a daily-Routine irrespective of busy lifestyle, to Have a Healthy Mind and Body, a person must take out some time in the Mornings. As soon as you, wake-up. - Saying "Thank You" (being Grateful and Thankful) for this Beautiful day. Practising Gratitude and being thankful for whatever you have (good health, relationships, career, finances and overall well-being) in your life for the first 5 minutes. Then must go for Brisk Walk in the Morning do Pranayama or Meditation for 15-20 mins. Then have a Healthy Breakfast and then go for your job/ workplace following a healthy start for the day. Then to live Healthy, physical Exercise is very necessary so people now Days have become aware and are Health Conscious and follow and have a Routine to go to gym and Work out (have become diet conscious too).

Sometimes, by doing everything and following a healthy Routine also, some people are having stress due to pressures and many are going into depression as unable to cope up with the stressful life. So, in such case when we are not well by going to Doctor's and we take Medication, so similarly do not hesitate to take a help of Counsellor and Psychiatrist - IF NEEDED.

As people are having the fear of being labelled and judged by Society, so they are not asking and seeking the guidance/help.

As Mental Health is equally very Important aspect and needs to be balanced with physical Health. So overall both the physical and mental Health needs to be balanced for a harmonious and healthy fit life. Taking care of our Health is our own Responsibility.

{As Health is Perfect, but sometimes it happens that some unpleasant mishappening and unfortunate Accidents happen, which are so unpredictable and unfortunate too (accidents are not in our hands). Sometimes the negligence of other person too can cause the unfortunate damage, which nobody is prepared for. (ACCIDENT)}

NOTE: AUTHOR'S OWN EXPERIENCE (My Own Experience)

Here I would like to share my own journey/ Experience (P-HEMA). Where I met with an Unfortunate accident. Here I am sharing this as today when I look back to that Incident of my Life. - I am just speechless but I have recovered completely. I am in my perfect Health now. As one fine morning when I was going to my office on my 2-wheeler, suddenly car came and hit my Vehicle and I fell down and straight on my back and Head and I was rushed to Hospital, as there were no internal-injury (head) found after MRI/ Scan, but I had multiple fractures in my "Spine". I was unable to move and it was that the Doctor's told me for spinal surgery. But I and my family were not ready for the Surgery, we told Doctor's that first we will show to some other Doctor and then take a decision (second opinion).

As time passed we were seeing that my mobility was not happening without help of some one as I needed help to get up - Walk and needed Support and then too I was on Bed for many months and my family was supportive and stood by me and were helping me through physiotherapy and medication.

But still the Recovery was not so much, as Doctor's had advised surgery. But I was not at all ready to undergo Surgery.

Here I am sharing this that during this time I was reading books of Self-Help and the Book written by Dr. Joe Dispenza.

(1) Becoming Super Natural.

(2) You are the Placebo.

(3) You can heal your life (by Louise Hay)

These books really Helped me and I also worked on my Mindset. Dr. Joe Dispenza also had spinal injury and he too recovered completely. So, then I was very much now sure that if he can heal, then I too can. I practised all the Methods, Meditation and Visualised -as told by him in the Book to the Core. Also, I watched the videos of Health & Mindset Coach.

Watching Health and Mindset videos, working on my Mindset, practising gratitude and Meditation and physiotherapy and exercise helped to recover completely without undergoing any surgery. I can now say from my personal Experience of my life, as I am a live example that I have healed completely and recovered without surgery.

Note: So, If I can do it anyone else can also, anyone who is facing something like this. It's my request that do not take a hasty decision by saying "Yes" to Surgery, As Surgery is recommended but should be the last-choice and option if everything fails, if nothing is working out then only say yes (but it is individual choice and in their hands to take decision what suits them the best this was just a suggestion).

The purpose to share this experience in the section of "HEALTH"–As I thought of adding this, as this is my personal experience and by sharing this may be helpful to many. Life is unpredictable.

NEVER GIVE UP……. KEEP GOING

"BELIEVE IN YOURSELF."

"IF I CAN – YOU TOO CAN"

So Healthy and being fit is the most Important aspect of everyone life at every phase of life. As after all the Best of the medication also sometimes people face health challenges that is why "Health is wealth". So, say thank you to that God/Divine who has blessed all of us with a healthy body where every organ is functioning properly and blessed with a Good Health and Healthy life. The Body is like a temple where we reside in, need to be taking care of it and also to maintain a healthy life-style as in today's hectic schedule of ours and routine our Lifestyle are the cause of many diseases, which are "life style diseases". (for example: Diabetes, blood pressure, obesity, stress, anxiety, thyroid, migraine and so many)

So, when a person is healthy - can Automatically focus on his workspace and when progressing in Career will have a Happy Relationships, with family and friends and this is how as it reflects and impacts on other and are very well interconnected. Thus, being healthy, can be full filling others aspects too and live Happy and Healthy Life.

HEALTH IS WEALTH,

So Be Healthy and Wealthy to live a happy and full filled life is a Goal of a human life!

The TIPS to Remain Healthy:

• Eat Healthy [Avoid Junk as much as possible]
(Eat Nutritious Balances food as possible).

• Exercise (Joining a Gym/Dance Zumba)
[Any Physical Activity – cycling, swimming, karate and yoga classes]

• MEDITATION – At least 10-15 mins sitting in silence.
meditate for 15 mins.

• Listen to Music
• Laughter [Laugh – watch comedy shows]
Laughter is the best Medicine.

• Spend some Time in Nature.
• Quality time, with family [Dinner Table]
Joyful Moments without phones.

• Go for a Regular Check - up (physical) once in a year.
• Have a balance - Emotional/physical fitness and stay spiritually connected with the divine.
• Good sleep...

B) RELATIONSHIP

We all need to live in a happy and harmonious relationships.

Most of the people are just neglecting their Relationships and mainly focusing on the external looks/Beauty and making money just to compete one-another and excel. But that does not make you a Successful person. The Real Success is how many lives did you touch.

How many people are happy because of you? Are you really responsible enough to make only. the livelihood and take care of your responsibilities by financially taking care of the needs or you are living life to live happily and make an impact as a good Human being by adding value to others life too.

Ask this to yourself:

MORNING - Where can I become a better Human being today? How I can become better Human-being today?

NIGHT (before sleep) - where did I become a better human being today?

It's okay if we do not find answers to these questions even If it is Smiling at Your Dinner and appreciate the chef.

By adding up little joy & happiness and bringing Smile on other's face and adding a hope into someone's eye also is a mark of a good human- being. Sometimes- giving your quality time to your old parents who took care of "you" and gave you the best upbringing, what are they asking is a little care, quality time with them is the biggest gift you can ever give to them. Everyone thinks that once they are grown-ups as adults giving money is only the responsibility of theirs towards elders – "parents". No, more than money again it's your valuable time and communication is one and only way to feel good and beautiful about yourself by making people feel good and beautiful about themselves"!

Do not be one role -Wonder or model is expanding the real meaning.

Definition of life' and have much broader definition that is not only being Successful but also Healthy, wealthy, loving, Caring, blissful, peaceful becoming a beautiful person from inside - out.

FOCUS on what you want to become, and be that CHANGE.

Focus on the champions of CHANGE.

Be a LEADER. Lead from the Front

Do not be a FOLLOWER.....

(SWACHH BHARAT ...... PROUD TO BE IN INDORE NUMBER 1 CLEAN CITY IN BHARAT)

In life everything and everyone cannot be according to us. Some will like and appreciate and some will dislike and criticize. If you want to really grow up by facing the stones which are thrown on you, just pick them up and build your castle.

I want to say is in life we do many things which are just a waste of time and still we continue doing so, as we are more inclined towards and focused on it and things are sometimes not in control.

Every moment you waste in life focusing on what you cannot control you missed as opportunity to focus on what you could have "controlled":

- People Resist/ change. Focus of the people even 1% also focus on them. You have to be the champion of the change.

Changes starts with one

So be that ONE.

If transforming your life, you have to bring the change in that Relationships". Be a Role Model that the coming generation will be able to emulate". Leaving a Legacy through your deeds and qualities so this is been carried by generation and generation to come in future.

Three things Required are for a Legendary Life (to leave a Legacy in this world)

Learn the art of building relationships, every relationship has its own unique blend and importance.

Three things required are:

Re-inventing yourself and evolving, leading.

REINVENT - EVOLVE – LEAD

We all are having a personal life which is our Family and Relatives and we have a professional Life and work place which in turn becomes a family only as we are spending most of our time with them, so we have a bond and connection with them too.

Maintaining a balanced Relationship is very important as we all are social animals and we need people to share and care. Any Relationship flourishes with these important needs.

a) Love

b) Kindness

c) Understanding [Mutual Understanding]

d) Harmony.

e) Respect for each other

f) Communication.

g) Trust

h) Support.

I) Care and Share (Caring and sharing).

Relationship can never be one-sided it has to be - give and take [Both ways] when we are born as human beings.

Relationship plays as important as "Spine".

Spine is the SUPPORT SYSTEM OF OUR BODY.

Maintaining healthy relationships are very important aspect of life.

In relationship

A Good Being → Balanced being is what matters.

JOY that you experience everything good that you hear for your kids - Appreciation and feeling PROUD of their qualities.

To your children (as father/mother parents are their world)

When father gave the Jig saw "Puzzle" to be solved to the child assembled the Jig-saw puzzle and got it right.

Jig- saw Puzzle - Assemble - I Got the Man the world become right.

Collectively we all are Right.

TURN EXPECTATION {Turn Expectations onto YOURSELF}

Asking self:

- Ask what value did you add to the family?
- In any Relationship what I can give,
- rather than what can-I receive?
- Be a 'Gift to the World'.
- Gift to Humanity

Whatever you are giving out in your relationships will come back to you.

Example: Country Measure in terms of Happiness

- Bhutan - Gross National happiness
- Dubai - Minister for Happiness" Happiness A Happier Dubai will be a gift to the world.

Ask yourself?

* How much Happiness can I add to everybody at Home?

"A Happy HOME" will bring happy relationships in the family. That is 'Togetherness'.

You become rich by what you give in your relationship. (love, happiness, joy, unity, share and care, support)

The richest way to live your life is to go into any relationship. What can I give ....?

BE A GIVER Always. (what you give, you receive)

- Be a giver of love

- Be a giver of Happiness

- Be A Giver of Respect

- Be A Giver of Kindness.

- Be A Giver of Positivity

DAY BY DAY IN EVERY WAY

I will be a "GIFT" (by adding value to others life in a positive way and contributing) to this world by being healthier, wealthy, loving, blissful, spiritual and caring.

A Human being has to make every day count, we are not given a day to waste it, but to construct a BETTER Tomorrow.

MAKING EVERYDAY OF YOUR LIFE "COUNT!"

Make Each DAY COUNT. (Meaningful, joyful, blissful)

Living a meaningful life, adding value to your relationship and strengthening bond which is living to the fullest.

Putting days into your life is 'AGEING'…….

* Are we only AGEING (age)?

* Are we growing and evolving with the AGE? Choice is in Your hands.

Let's keep growing by putting life into everyday of our life.

The day you are not useful to the world - You do not exist and matter, but just Breathing through this body (that is not real existence).

Everyday let's use ourselves with a sense of purpose to serve and add value to our loved ones, friends/family, to this society and be useful to this beautiful world.

Day by day in every way - Man of all the creations of God has been designed to be a "Holistic Wonder" and not a one role wonder. Your Success in one role of your life, does not permit you to fail in the other roles of your life.

You can be an Extraordinary family man and still have your social obligations and responsibilities.

You need to be playing multiple roles and cannot be playing just one role.

"Only a Balanced Life is a Complete Life".

Day By Day in Every way by becoming a better version of self and evolving in every aspect. To live a "Purposeful life" Human being is evolving Consciously (evolving consciousness).

I will be a gift to the world day by day in every way, I will be a gift to the world by becoming…..a balanced person in every aspect of life.

The greatest gift of being as an 'human being' can be -TODAY of our lives is Better than "YESTERDAY".

Every Tomorrow can be better than Today.

The greatest Joy of every HUMAN- BEING is that you are an Evolving consciousness. (Everyday learning something new through your experiences you are evolving as a better version of self).

{You learn –> You grow -> You evolve}.

OUR VEDA SAYS: "Jeevaatma came from Paramatma".

But science says that a - Human Being is a 'Bio magnetic field that descended from cosmic magnetic field.

Have an Abundant Mindset.

Become an Abundant Minded. Be a GIFT to the world by becoming:

➤ Healthy

➤ Wealthy

➢ Loving

➢ Blissful

➢ Spiritual

Balancing and growing through all the above aspects. Having a holistic approach towards life.

- healthy

This Vehicle (our body) is the greatest Gift of God on to us, and let's use it to serve the world, the only way your body can serve you, if you take care of the body. So, for that being healthy is utmost important aspect to serve (self and others).

- WEALTHY

Financial Abundance in the hand of a Good Human being will help building a happy and better family, better society and help in creating and building a better world. On the other Hand of financial Abundance in the hand of a bad Human being will destroy the world. So, there is only one way we can save this world from Bad People that is all

Note: Here bad people mean indulging in wrong practice and activities Bad People should become poor and there is only one way by which bad people can become poor is that all the good people should become rich and successful.

- LOVING

Take Love Beyond your relationships- Love nature Love Environment, Love Animals, Love Each other - love People, Spread Love…… Love is the way to live.

- BLISSFUL

We Need a Happy World, in a happy world we don't fight with each other, Happy people don't fight, living in harmony. We all need a happier world. Be enthusiastic, be energetic, be exuberant, be demonstrative. Bring happiness wherever you are. Bring Bliss, wherever you are. Wear a smile on your face every day. Live a blissful life.

- SPIRITUAL

Meditation is the connection of your inner being to the universal supreme power.

Meditation is appointment with GOD but most of the people don't have time?

All your Disappointments in your life is because you do not have time for an appointment with God (supreme power).

A part of you, should always be connected to that divine.

Always feel spiritually connected to the great force!

Apart from Meditation, prayers are also the way to connect to God.

I want to quote this here

Example:

Ravindranath Tagore": (poet) said

A world that is not broken up by the fragments, by narrow domestic walls into that heaven of freedom.

My father let my country Awake [In a world that is not broken up into fragments]

A world beyond DISCRIMINATION.

(As we are all living in a world of discrimination).

WE NEED ONE WORLD (TOGETHERNESS)

WE ALL ARE ONE,

"So together let's make this world a beautiful place to live".

EVERYDAY MATTERS: make every day count

How you live everyday matters.

A person (Dincharya) ~ Daily Routine.

Today we say one thing very commonly, said in today's busy world that is

"WE ARE BUSY.............."

- 'WE DON'T HAVE TIME'

Everything has a Time to do, you don't have Time - For Exercise, time to sit in Silence, time to pray, time to spend with your family and friends, time to develop new skills, time for self- care, time for social gatherings and spiritual gatherings and events (family get together and social get together)...........and many more to go on for which everyone is making an easy excuse "DON'T HAVE TIME"................

Everything that is a "Time-Pass "we all do it by time and Everything that is important, we don't have time for it, for exercise you don't have time, exercise to become Healthy and Fit.

Choosing your priorities…………..

• Are your priorities really right?
Setting your priorities and taking out your precious time is what the most of us are not really doing, and setting our priorities in a mindful way and prioritising our daily activities is missing in today's hectic life and schedules.

• Family time
Can you take care of your Body?

Do you take out time for yourself ?……..no time

➢ Few minutes of silence Everyday – no time

➢ Meditation- no time

➢ Exercise-no time

➢ Brisk walk -no time

"EVERYTHING HAS A TIME"

We should all have a time for everything and do everything in time. (self-care and self-discipline).

["A TIME FOR EVERYTHING AND EVERYTHING IN ITS TIME"]

Cultivate the discipline of Time - to allocate time for Everything that is essential.

Discipline- what is important for me and doing it by prioritising that in life.

Reinventing self…… Evolving and growing, every day in every way.

The basis of every Relationship now has shifted from "EMOTIONS" to information which means.

"This is what you need to working on yourself" not only with your family, colleagues within another organisation.

But also in your parenting……. also in your marriage… in creating an organization everywhere this is the basis which means-

The new way of living is this:

THAT ON WHICH YOU INVEST TIME AND

COMMUNICATION GROWS……

THAT WHICH YOU DO NOT GIVE YOUR TIME AND COMMUNICATION WILL SHRINK AND FADE AWAY (collapse).

If there is a gap – that is not investing time and Communication in that particular Relationship. (Spouse, Son, Father, Mother, friend or anyone whom you are, close too and whom so ever).

So, whatever, age you are in between 20+ years and above each and every Relation and relationship has its own fragrance and quality, and it has to be nurtured in its unique way. But the most important factors in any Relationship are these two:

INVEST IN TIME & COMMUNICATION

Investing in Quality Time.

1)   TIME – Spending quality Time.

Taking out Quality Time and spending with your loved ones and family is utmost important. It is not the quantity, but the quality that bonds a relationship and flourishes.

2) COMMUNICATION - To communicate in a proper and right way and communication has to be two ways always. It has to be that one talks and other listens and then the one who is listening will respond.

Relationships have to be built

"PEOPLE ARE WITH YOU WHETHER TIMES ARE GOOD OR TIMES ARE BAD. THOSE ARE CALLED REAL RELATIONSHIPS "

Adding quality to your relationships by nurturing them with – Understanding, Trust and Genuine care.

Let's fill our lives with small sparks of positivity and happiness, while these moments may not erase our negativity and pain, but surely can give us the strength to face any situation and overcome them with grace.

* WHERE ARE YOU INVESTING YOUR TIME?

Where are you giving your attention and spending more time

- On Social Media.

- Instagram.
- WhatsApp
- Other social media platforms.

Relationship means reinventing every aspect of your life and maintaining a balance and harmony, living to the fullest. Adding value and contributing.

- Evolution -evolving as a better human being through your life experiences.

Every Human being Evolves with time will you drink water from dirty tumbler? No

Will you Eat in a dirty plate? No

Will you use a dirty washroom

outside? No

We human being will not use anything dirty, then ask yourself this question Today?

* How do you expect Divinity to descend into you, if you from inside are dirty?

(divinity will not reside in you if you are dirty from inside)

(Dirty means - Having Jealous, Hatred, envious, anger, Insecure, greed, lust etc) from inside"

Asking to Yourself you want Evolve?

*AM I BECOMING A BETTER AND BEAUTIFUL HUMAN BEING FROM INSIDE EVERY DAY OF MY LIFE?

Beautiful being means not from the external look but how beautifully you have evolved adding meaning to your life, by balancing all the aspects of your life.

"The Art of Building Beautiful Marriage":

Choosing your life-Partner.

Men are from mars.

Women are from Venus.

As they say – "opposite always attract"

What should be attractive to one another should be their qualities more than the external looks.

As the focus today is more on external looks while choosing the partner not their qualities.

Marriage is to be practised on Earth, two people coming together from a different family, backgrounds. (Environment/culture)

Marriage means - 2 wheels of Life (2-wheeler) travelling together on the path of life together, "balancing" both the WHEELS" of 2-wheeler.

"One wheel is you and the other wheel is your life partner "- A beautiful partnership for life-time together accepting each other the way they are.

The way you understand each other and express your emotions and love (Expression of love) towards one-another and respecting each other feelings and moral values and giving space.

As the Role of Parents is to find a Right and suitable companion and partner for their children (male or female).

So, the family chooses on behalf, keeping the overall well-being of the two families in "Arrange Marriage".

But as the world is changing and the overall thought process and mindset too have been evolving from generation to generation - Now the Youth are preferring to choose and Decide their partner according to their likes [Do not want parents to choose on behalf of them]. This is in "Love Marriage".

- In Arranged Marriage
First they get married, and then try to understand each other and then fall in Love with each other.

- In Love Marriage
First they choose and understand and then get married, keeping their likes and priorities in mind. [Now a days, most of the Marriages are Love Marriages]

A marriage is a "COMMITMENT" of two FAMILIES. This Decision is the most Important Decisions of Life, so keeping the Two families. [both the sides] so many people are coming together as it is not just the Overall, status/Looks/Appearance, education and social status.

But it is a "Companionship" and Partnership of Two families. Their Moral Values/Upbringing

Their qualities → Nature/Behaviour and Social Background should be focussed on to in this Partnership.

Now days the Marriage too has become so fragile and Unpredictable in many of the cases - The main reason that in today's world. Everyone wants everything INSTANT.

To fall in Love-Instantly "Love at First Sight"

Divorce and separation at "First Fight"

The Main Reasons why the Divorce percentage is growing exponentially is because of these Reasons:

1) Lack of Patience. (Anger/Aggression/fights)

2) Lack of Quality Time.

3) Lack of Communication.

4) Lack of Compatibility

5) Lack of Trust/faith

6) Influence Technology/ Social Media & films

7) Ego and Superiority Complex

8) Attitude and Behaviour

The focus should not be "in competing" with each other as both are working [Professional life] the professional Life and the Personal Life is Imbalanced due to Lack of 'quality time'. As both the partners are not having enough time to understand each other.

Accepting each other's strengths and weaknesses (Accepting the IMPERFECTIONS makes this partnership beautiful and meaningful).

No one is perfect. But to accept those imperfections and move forward............'TOGETHER'.

It is our reaction to the situation or circumstances makes our lives comfortable or miserable. Life will not be the same as sometimes there are deep clouds of troubles/odd and sometimes sunshine.

Learning through the experiences and challenges and to overcome them.

Always be ready to face life as it comes (good or bad) what it throws as sometimes in one's life journey - we must not give up, irrespective of the challenges and rewards, we must look with positive attitude and learn from the experiences - the lessons of 'life is a Biggest Teacher'.

The life teaches the toughest lessons – learn from it and evolve.

We all learn and grow and Evolve through our journey Life keeps on teaching you until you Learn your "LESSONS".

So, learn them and evolve and keep growing in positive direction.

4 PILLARS

There are 4 pillars in our life at every stage of our lives and everyone needs all of them and they are:

1) Love

2) Happiness

3) Support (caring and sharing)

4) Understanding

Why I am saying 4 pillars because we as Humans have feelings, emotions and thoughts and as we are living life, our life requires love in our relationship and meant to be happy fulfilled and content, and we are also Social animals means that we need someone to be with us who will look after us and take care, also love us as we are emotional beings.

This I am saying because if the foundation and pillars are strong the building will be stronger enough and face the challenges and overcome them easily as pillars are laid strong, but most often, we see that in our lives., some or other important thing is missing, in life what is missing and how can it be fulfilled by bridging up the gaps, and the sad part is everyone knows it, but no one does it - who is going to Bridge Up that gap, which is missing in their life. It's your own responsibility to bridge up the gap, as nobody will come to bridge up. Take responsibility of your life in your hands as – 'it's your life and you have to live it'. Are you ready to bridge up the gap? that is missing and make an Impact in a positive way. As mentioned do take some time to reflect upon that what has been the one most important aspect that is impacting and missing in life. At times it can be more than one aspect which is missing. Is it love or support or understanding or money or career or health or some other reasons.

In such situation, we need to take responsibility of our lives and do think upon, that what really went wrong and where did it go wrong? Being wrong is one big opportunity the life has given you is learning from the mistakes and make them the stepping stones of your life. Often everyone is some stages of life have definitely made mistakes, but the sad part of it is that they did forget to learn from that mistake….. they MIS….TO TAKE and learn from it.

{The most successful people we see have not become successful overnight, but they made mistakes failed again started then again failed but again learnt from it and then again they tried and again failed, but they kept trying and did not give up on the path they choose and finally succeeded and thus they are successful and are big names today }.If I start to name than the list will continue and not end but we only see their success but forget to see the journey and the path they have walked. So, to be successful need to balance all the aspects and move in the direction towards your destination that is your goal and dreams.

As I am sharing this I want to just say and remember that just when pandemic hit the world, the entire world had to face and some people grew in this difficult phase but wherein some gave up, lost everything. This was the biggest Lessons that we all got in life that we cannot be taking everything for Granted. Be prepared for uncertainties, as when the world was standstill, and people did not know, what to do and how to do?

Biggest lesson we all had to learn the lessons of life, grow from the negative situations and experiences by overcoming with grace.

Health /Relationships/Career/Money everything was a Priority then.

Many lost their loved ones, many are still facing some health issues after effects of pandemic, many of them lost their job, Businesses were shut down with losses.

C) CAREER:

As each one of us are unique and have talents and skills, based on that we choose over education and then make that as our profession and career. On the Basis what you have chosen to do in your life, that is on what you are doing for your livelihood and living and choosing your career and building it is in your hand. As after the Education and taking the Degree and Masters and then you start to be independent by earning. As you have to be financially Independent. As we all are living by earning for our bread and butter.

Do you want to make your Career by following and doing what you like to do, and you have chosen that profession as pursuing that as your career too. Sometimes in life many teenagers and youngsters are so confused that they are unable to decide what, stream of Education to choose and pursue career in that, as the parents on behalf of them have chosen that career path for their kids. They have their own aspirations - Dreams and Desire, which they want to be fulfilled through their children and then they are not even seeing the interest of the young minds and expect their children to just blindly pursue what is chosen for them as they think that as elders and well- wishers they are always right and they know better can take and make right choices and decisions being parents/ elders, and also assume that this is 'best' for them. In this Competitive world every parent wants the best and thinks that they have to Excel in this competition. Here sometimes the Young Minds (YOUTH) at times are unable to face the pressures and take extreme steps and which results in ending up……

Note: *Do not take extreme steps irrespective of the situation.

Instead of this » One can be courageous enough to open out their heart and speak and communicate to Parents/Elders/ Counsellor's and seek their guidance as they unable to take this pressure and require an alternative option, so they can have an choice what options can further go better on their behalf which they are liking also and can give up their best - which they can now pursue and make this as their further new approach towards dealing, with what they are presently coping up with.

As we come across now a day many youngsters are failing to actually take a right decision for themselves and instead of that they just keep doing and facing it keeping everything within them. Which in fact many times leads to mental illness, stress, Anxiety - Depression and finally end up without any solutions and drastically impacting the lives. We all are knowing what to do but sometimes don't know how to do? In such phases of your career where you are unable to acting on right time with corrective measures can truly be a turning point into your career perspective.

As I remember, one of my students, during her stages of choosing a right path and field for her studies and career and was pressurised from parents to choose the career which was not the choice of my student. My student wanted to pursue something else, so she came to me and told and shared that what she was looking for and wanting to pursue and build further, but she unable to express her opinion and her choices to parents, as they were not listening, so in that phase as a turning point in her life, I took the liberty as her Teacher and also Career Counsellor and Life Coach approached to their Parents and put across her strengths and her Talents in which she wanted to make her career into, and finally like what was the magical Shift and change was she changed her stream and pursued her passion. Then she was pursuing initially for her CA Studies, opted to change and pursued Interior Designing and completed successfully and today is a very successful Interior Designer.

3C's OF THE LIFE:

Choices, Chances, Changes

You must make a choice, to take a chance if you want anything in life to change.

Also in Movie 3 idiots, we saw that an engineer wanted to become a Photographer and finally pursued his passion and made Successful career,

As they say -

"IF YOU FOLLOW YOUR PASSION

MONEY AND SUCCESS WILL FOLLOW YOU"

So, my request to all the Youth irrespective of the male or female don't compare yourself with anyone else as each one has a uniqueness within us, so instead of copying and following someone else, do follow your heart and do what you are good at.

Career is important as we have to make our Identity as well recognition through what we are doing in professional Front. It may be a 9 to 5 JOB in a Corporate world or MNC or a businessman/business woman or an entrepreneur or to have your own START UP's.

It's your choice which is in your hand and mind, Choose wisely.

Just don't do anything because the world is doing, do only that which you feel you are good at and wanting to do and give your 100 % into it.

To excel in your field.

At every stage of our life, we have experiences and situations but based on those experiences you are sometimes making mistakes too, but always can learn the LESSONS from your mistakes and Grow from those and make them as stepping Stones in your life. In this fast Technological World, the world is Evolving so fast and you have so many choices in this Era where everything is just at the Touch off a button. The Artificial Intelligence (AI) and Digital world has made so much advancement in each and every field. We have wide spectrum to choose, what suits you and your Professional Life the Best that is totally in your hand and in your mind.

BE THE CREATOR OF YOUR OWN LIFE……… AND CREATE THE BEST ONE.

Don't just work for Living or making a livelihood, but make such choice which will give you the Satisfaction and money and success too, where you have infinite opportunities to grow and flourish and live to your highest potential. I through my experiences can tell you one thing choosing a RIGHT CAREER FOR LIVING LIFE, ENJOYING IT COMPLETELY, AND ALSO BECOMING FINANCIALLY INDEPENDENT IS THE ULTIMATE GOAL.

DONT WORK TO LIVE BUT LIVE TO WORK………

FOLLOW YOUR PASSION AND CONVERT YOUR PASSION INTO YOUR CAREER....

You will be successful and Happy, satisfied too. Sometimes many youths have multi talent, so if they want they can also have a side Hustle by following it alongside with their mainstream. Today's world "Multiple sources of Income" should be the way of living.

TIPS:

- Choose what you want to pursue (career/ profession)
- Always follow your Passion.
- Do not change your Career path again and again. (changing jobs and changing streams)
- Have a Progressive Approach towards your career
- Build a Side Hustle.

D) MONEY

In the entire journey of life apart from family, culture and values money plays the most important aspect in everyone's life.

From the time we are been born and till the time we are living our lives as human's all our needs and wants have been fulfilled and taken care by this 5-letter word which is 'M O N E Y…..'

It is very evident historically that money has been instrumental in developing individuals and family well-being on day-to-day basis. Money helps us to meet our basic needs mainly to buy food and shelter to pay for education and healthcare.

Money helps in balancing happiness in families leading to a positive and healthy lifestyle which in turn individuals to think on managing their family welfare as well act as security for their future. We all need money for having stable financial foundation which reduces stress and worries - it acts as a safety net.

Every individual or family always aspire to live a normal, healthy and stable life by pursuing their goals in quality education also to pursue other hobbies and pursue their passions. To have good health care planning in good investments also to have planning good quality time with their families in form of vacations and other future investments (financial security).

So, we can sum it as:

M – Monetise for growth

O – Opportunities

N – Never give up on your dreams and goals

E – Ensuring stability

Y – Your thought process to stabilise lifestyle

Many of us have seen people managing on basis of their earnings and at the same time there are individuals who have everything but due to their negligence towards importance of money, negative practices, not thinking about future of self as well their families for which sometimes lack of financial commitment and planning the consequences have to be owned by the family. The dependence in this case has no mistakes but still pay for the mistakes done by someone else without having financial plans and goals in their life. So here what I want to tell is irrespective of the social status we all as individuals need to be financially independent and not to depend on others and take the responsibilities of our own life by being financially independent so as to meet the needs of life. By not blaming others and being self - responsible is in our hand.

WE ALWAYS HAVE A CHOICE

3 C'S OF LIFE

CHOICES YOU MAKE, CHANCES YOU TAKE, CHANGES YOU OPT

(Life always give chances, but many fail to make changes, leaving no choices.)

"YOU MUST MAKE A CHOICE, TO TAKE A CHANCE IF YOU WANT ANYTHING IN LIFE TO CHANGE".

Be the CHANGE.

Money helps in understanding the economics of growth and helps us to find good arenas to grow. For example, this kind of opportunities to grow with help of money, people plan their future of children's education and career, plan for good policies of healthcare, planning of purchasing their own house, plan for vehicles, plans for future securities through various financial investments – mutual funds, stocks, gold investments, real–estate, to live a wealthy and satisfied life. As a youth we need to start to plan our future at the right time, at the right age, so that as we grow and retire we can enjoy and reap the fruits while living a happy, healthy and fulfilled life (Maintaining financial balance and family is utmost important as a youth to be responsible as a citizen, as a human being and balancing the main aspect "MONEY".)

Money plays a vital role as it reflects and impacts the other areas as health, relationships, career also.

There are many instances of individuals planning with help of money allows them to do charity, helping people for their basic needs, helping in making old-age homes, charity hospitals, community marriages and donations to religious institutions, organising health camps, blood camps and free health check–ups.

All the above derive the importance of money at all aspects of life journey as well indirectly contribute to the nation.

MY SUGGESTION:

My suggestion to all the youngsters (youth) is to understand their family values and understand the importance of valuing money by having financial plannings and investment starting at a young age so that as you grow, your money and investments also grows. Start saving and investing at every level wherever possible which will help to stabilise their future and live a happy, healthy and wealthy life.

CHAPTER 5

THE SECOND INNINGS OF LIFE (50 + AND ABOVE) AND OLD AGE

As those are the truly blessed ones who in this beautiful journey have crossed the milestone of the number 50 years of their beautiful journey celebrating and living this beautiful life every day in every way growing and evolving as a beautiful human being crossing through the various phases of life and cherishing this phase as now to celebrate the "GOLDEN JUBLIEE" with your happy family, relatives, friends, celebrating life.

CELEBRATE LIFE

Live to the fullest, life is a celebration and now celebrations in life

- Celebration of love is "relationship".
- Celebration of your blessings is "happiness" that is to celebrate more and more what you have in life that is the manifestation of this happiness.
  Happiness is the celebration of blessings in your life.
- Celebration of god is faith that is divine force is always working along with you.
- Celebration of your potential is called success.

Each one of us are differently capable and unique, you have been be-stored with unique capabilities, and potential that you have added value and contributed to the family, society and to this beautiful world.

This is the phase where now you can think of relaxing and retiring from the hectic and monotonous rhythmic life by taking a pause and giving yourself the time to enjoy and cherish every moment by taking care of yourself and your family and now you are ready to take a retirement from your professional front and give some time cherishing the moments and valuing them by living everyday with your children and grandchildren and enjoy this beautiful phase of life which very few are blessed with to cherish and live these moments in life, though you have been retired from your professional life but now at a personal front you have been promoted as a head of the family in your family tree and becoming a grandfather/grandmother and taking this step ahead in your life through this beautiful journey where you are reaping the fruits and enjoying this beautiful phase.

As they say that though you get tired but you cannot retire at your personal front. Although you have retired from the professional front in this second phase but enjoy now by living a relaxed and taking care of self, health and family.

As you have grown through this journey you require some rest, so retired phase is a most beautiful phase as now you have time for yourself - meditation, going for a brisk walk, spending time with your age group circle in parks, spiritual celebrations and gatherings, going to some yoga retreats also making spiritual trips to spiritual pilgrimages - connecting to the divine through prayers.

Seeing your children grow and becoming a grandparent (grandfather and grandmother) as they too are growing now and in your family tree you are the head of the family been promoted as grandfather/grandmother and your thriving family.

This phase is the "SECOND INNINGS" of life as crossing the age of 50 which provides immense happiness seeing your children and grandchildren grow and evolve.

In this age when you have travelled through this journey living your life in a best way and beautiful way as only few are blessed to live this journey, living and flourishing, seeing the generations to grow and witnessing it by living every moment what could life have been given more than this blessing that you have that opportunity to celebrate the 50 years of partnership with the spouse, 50 years of a wedding anniversary celebration where the entire family is witnessing this beautiful and everlasting moments with friends and family the beautiful journey you have lived celebrating and enjoying this journey to the fullest.

As in this journey we all have come on this earth and we all know the day we were born that is our date of birth (DOB) but now we are not knowing the day we will be leaving this planet earth (date of exit) but blessed are those who have happily lived their life and crossed 50+, 60+, 70+, 80+ and so on............... what could have been asked more for, as you are truly blessed are those ones who are been cherishing this milestones and witnessing a journey, witnessing a world – from writing letters to emails/WhatsApp, from landlines to computers and mobile phones, from open theatres to multiplex, from coal engines to bullet trains, from bullock cart to space/satellites that is not only you have seen and have witnessed the technological revolution but also seen human evolution.

While telling the grandchildren the stories of your era and generation now you are seeing that your grandchildren are holding the technological gadgets in their hands telling and teaching how to operate and use, not only you're teaching to your grandchildren but learning from them now (technologically). What a journey you have lived from then to now enjoying every aspect of life and living to the fullest, this phase of your journey.

As once you were young-raised your children (upbringing) now that your children and your grandchildren are taking care of you physically, mentally and emotionally. The roles have been reversed. Where in, you have lived your journey and living it to the fullest, living a fulfilled and a healthy long life.

"LIFE IS A JOURNEY – ENJOY IT"

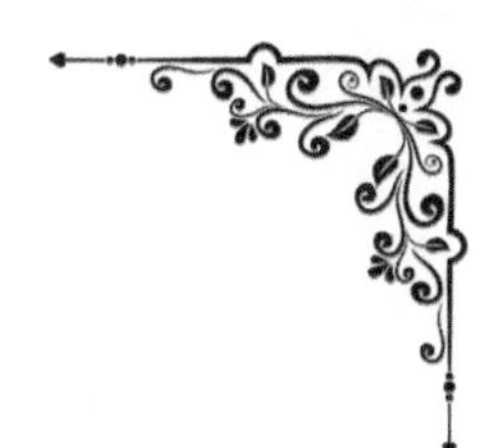

THE CYCLE OF LIFE

FROM THE AUTHOR

In this coming book "The Journey Of Life", I have penned my thoughts and beliefs in bringing across the soul life cycle of individuals at different phases of life . As Life is a precious gift of god to us , life is all about learning and growing each day and every day. We all have our own unique journey, how are we living this life by adding value and meaning to life is in our hands. Live life to the fullest.

We learn while living life.

Life is an endless journey between dreams and reality.

I believe strongly this book might help many in understanding their journey of life.

Life is a beautiful journey …….. Enjoy it!

www.ingramcontent.com/pod-product-compliance
Lightning Source LLC
Chambersburg PA
CBHW021113130726
47988CB00003B/999